The Way Of Things

Poems by Shannon Vesely

Rogue Faculty Press

Nebraska

Grateful acknowledgement is made to the editors of the following publications in which these poems first appeared, and to the institutions which supported the writing of these works:

Nebraska Life, *Davis County Psalms*, *Sanctuaries*, Brush Creek Foundation for the Arts, Kimmel Harding Nelson Center for the Arts.

First Edition

Cover art by Calvin Banks
Author photo by Shannon Vesely

Printed in the USA on acid-free paper.
To order online, go to *amazon.com*

Table of Contents

After The Rain 1

Morning Glory 2

My Shadow 3

Say You Are Certain About These Things 4

Summer Tanagers 5

Naming The Flowers 6

The Way Of Things 8

Beneath The Willow 10

To A Dying Classmate 12

Young Wife, Custer County, Nebraska 1912 14

Night Sky 19

Wild Clover 20

Prayer For The Fawns 21

Bubble Boy 22

Catching A Wave 24

For Griffin, Almost Five 25

Honeysuckle Berries 26

School Drop-Off 27

Song Of The Cottonwoods 28

So This Is Joy 29

The Leap 30

The Sailors Of Cinque Terre 31

What Will Hold 32

Witching Hour At Lake Wapello 33

Swinging 34

The Smallest Girl 35

To My Mother On Her 86th Birthday 37

Fireflies 39

From the Air 40

House Of Common Prayer 41

Marmalade Moon 42

My Mother's Raincoat 43

On A Second Viewing Of The Pieta 45

Photo Shoot 47

Good Planks 48

Deliverer 49

Tree Rut 50

The River Of Cottonwoods 51

The Day The Indigo Bunting Showed Up 52

Sumac 53

The Passion Of November 54

Sunrise, Late September 55

Late Autumn, Southern Iowa 56

Last Mowing 57

Cardinal In Late Winter 58

Sierra Madre Range, Wyoming 60

Round Bales 61

All The Best Things 62

Goldfinch In Winter 63

April Day 64

Apple Blossom Time 65

Love Story 66

End Roll 67

We Would Be Poorer 68

About the Author 70

Acknowledgements 71

To My Mother and Father

After The Rain

The oak leaves are salamanders.
Slick with dew, they slither through first light
on amphibious lobes.
They blink slowly,
their membranes drinking in the dappled day.

Today, I crawl from the mud,
into this geography I once knew—
both land and water, both me and you.

But older now, I am a pilgrim again.
I move with caution,
feeling my green way into the arbor, fearing
I have no gills to go on.

Yet, above is the land of the leaf-salamander
where both/and is always the answer,
and where the whole wet world warms
to the day.

Morning Glory

Twice, the morning glory has climbed the trellis
sending each tine instinctively
into intricate patterns of loop and curl,
loop and curl.

And in spite of the calligraphy of green
that sends it horizontally into the cedars,
it climbs.

How can it know?
How can it imagine this perfect bud-to-be?
And how can it feel the burst of blue,
its deep sapphire edges
and violet throat?

And why, season after season,
does it begin again?

My Shadow

An hour after dawn,
my shadow stretches proprietarily along the road
blackening the sunny mounds of trefoil
and the burnished wings of finches.
Its legs are dark trunks.
Across the seas of first light,
its torso spreads like a continent of shame,
while its head, a hapless tectonic plate,
settles over a mantle of shoulders.

Its appetite knows no end:
bridal heads of Queen Anne's Lace
scarlet crests of cardinals,
dew-glazed grass, maple saplings—
it stuffs them all into its burgeoning belly.

Now as the sun streaks through the trees
lighting up the orchid petals of cone flowers,
it blunders forward—leaden, determined,
the worst of me.

Even as morning christens the world,
it holds the road
and will not move aside.

Say You Are Certain About These Things

the freckled light that swims in spring puddles
the sound of snow geese ruffling the fields
the single mulberry in your hand
the words *murmur* and *water*

Say you are certain enough to give them
to the doubters,
all this lovely clarity tumbling into the glass
through which others have only seen darkly.

This would really be something.
This could change the world—
or at least change this day.
And a day may be just enough to coax
the triflers from the shallows.

A day when the dawn breaks with bluster and blow
and certainty is a magnificent tail wind.
A day when you take to the road,
peddling your finest wares:
a robin's egg here, a verse there;
a month of tulips, an ivory whisper.

Say that you're certain enough about all these things
to stake your life on them.

Summer Tanagers

live deep within the timber.
At dusk, they call to each other
warbling to welcome the night.

If you stand silently near the timber's edge,
you might see one:

a blood-orange jewel lying in the hollow
just at the base of summer's throat.

Or you might follow their love songs into the treetops—
blinking and refocusing,
scanning and rescanning,

to no avail.

Perhaps another time
when the sun is just beginning to set
and the last light floods a pocket in the upper story
where a single tanager sits.

Perhaps a moment when you forget
to try, when you simply look up
and there, on the limb of a young linden,
a summer tanager sits.

Or perhaps a dream
in which your lover calls out to you,
his heart a blood-orange beacon
in the dark.

Naming The Flowers

I was born for this job,
but I came too late,
the delphinium and dahlia
having already turned their petals to the sun,
their histories written.

Astilbe, an Old World daughter,
had reigned an empire of woodlands
by the time I had spoken my first words.

And I can accept this on most days.
On days when crocus push through spring snow,
when lilac branches bend under purple weight,
then it's enough just to be in the presence
of such wonder.

But the coral bells and stargazer lilies,
the morning glories and sweet peas—
I should have been there to write these names in the book,
my letters like inky petals across the page,
a calligraphy of top notes on the breeze.

And the honeysuckle, oh the white *parfum* of it!
I should have been there to speak its name
into a world that had never known such scent.

I have been too late for many things—
for naming and for knowing,
for loving.
When the party was over,

the floor littered with regret,
I've stood at the door and wept.

But when I showed up late for your life,
when all your days had been boxed and laureled
and the earth had taken you in,
this was unconscionable.

If I had been there at the beginning,
I would have named you gladiolus
or chrysanthemum, something glorious—

I would have knelt before the book of names
my heart's nib trembling before your open page.

The Way Of Things

As the sun slips below the ridge,
the day dissolves into the tree line,
a smudge pot of coral
then the palest yellow and near-blue.

In the cabin, I look out at the timber.
I can barely see the white tips of his antlers
pierce the dusk.
When he moves, he parts the nettles.
He makes a way, this young buck,
his dun-slicked back like the hull of a cargo ship
pushing the night forward.

It's the way of things:
this pushing the next thing forward,
the inevitable, first as a suggestion
and then as a thing of its own.

It's the way of things:
the darkness on a steady course,
time its lodestar.

For in the blink of an eye,
the day who spent the hours with such abandon—
light and color painting the world with such a broad and lovely
brush—
succumbs.

Then the buck beds down in the cedar thicket
and the hills tremble with coyotes.
Cold so clear it shines
crowns the world.

But in the blink of an eye,

the thickets stir again.
The hills simmer all golden and garnet,
and every stone is jeweled with frost.

It's the way of things:
the day refusing to die,
germinating in the ash heap
and promising—like a sleeping seed—
its return.

Beneath The Willow

Not much grows beneath the willow.
Its leafy umbrella keeps out the sun,
so that the earth beneath it is moist
and barren.
Even the fungi have turned up their noses
at this spot, where light is always
compromised.

On the best days, the sun dapples a way
through branches which skim the earth
like a processional train.

But make no mistake:
there is an entire world here
beneath the willow.
You would know this if you push aside the green curtain
and enter.
Once there, your eyes—as eyes will—
struggle to adjust to the darkness of a summer afternoon.

But take the advice of one who has lived a thousand lifetimes there:
you do not need eyes to see what you have come to see.
So close your eyes.
It matters little—eyes open or closed—in this world
beneath the willow tree.

Outside, the sun shines as it must,
calling the blossoms and hours into sharp focus,
and the day inches on
fraught with duty.

But beneath the willow tree,
you can try on different lives,
casting aside the rumpled remnants of one

in favor of another.

Here, you can do-over
and over.

Here, you can paint the sky apricot
and offer your heart, as open as a summer meadow,
to a world that always receives it
tenderly.

Here, the darkness is a feather bed
in which you can lay your weary worries,
and the *oughts* and *musts* have voices so small
that they are drowned in song.

Beneath the willow tree,
each day breaks in delirium,
a joy so generous that even the dirt
smiles.

So pass by if you will.
Give the willow a nod as you speed
towards somewhere.

As for me,
I will spend a thousand lifetimes here,
each one more splendid than the last.

To A Dying Classmate

Four hundred miles away, you convalesce.
Your fingers, now wafers,
flake into transparent pieces which fall soundlessly
like scales upon your bed clothes.
And your hands, which have already begun to leave this world,
cannot hold a pen.
So today, the clear-eyed nurse with the child's voice
holds a pen over a sheet of notebook paper
and waits.
This is the pen she tucks behind her ear,
the pen that records daily medications,
blood pressure readings and bowel movements.
So what would you have her write?

What news do you have to share in a friendly letter
to a classmate who has walked her morning miles
and sits drinking coffee as she looks over
the sunlit timber?
What news but that you are dying—
one wretched piece by one wretched piece.
That your home is an empty tomb
that no longer waits for your return
and that, as they spoon oatmeal into your mouth,
you taste the coming autumn,
the way it gives itself—leaf by leaf—
to death.
What words do you send from your sick bed
whose geography is the only land you know?

And then the clear-eyed nurse speaks
saying, *Let's tell her about the residents' luau last weekend.*
Let's tell her about how you wore a yellow lei and drank punch
while someone's grandson played the ukulele.
As she speaks, she pens big, loopy words

which festoon the page.
Pleased, she folds the finished letter
and seals the envelope.

There we go, she says,
all done.
And there it is.
A surer proclamation has not been made.

All done:
this life without legs and lungs
that must be narrated now by another.

Yet when you close your eyes,
you are walking in a field,
trailing your fingers over the burnished tips of foxtail.
And the autumn air is bright and sweet
as a ripe plum.

Young Wife, Custer County, Nebraska, 1912

1

The world outside her window looks in.
Stone-eyed, framed and frozen,
it is just as she imagines
winter should be:

the white bark of hickory,
a few nests of dead leaves,
and a horizon as pale
as the last breath of autumn.

And she lives here
just as she imagines a wife should:
framed in this dark box of December,
the edges of her mouth fluttering in the cold,
the dreams of her feet fixed
to a stern perimeter.

Who would hear her heart heave
and list in the wind?
And who would dare hold it,
this songless, beating thing that pumps as it must
night and day?

If this were a Russian tale,
she would take the hand of a fine young officer
and they would walk along the Neva River
where stars punctuate the blue-black sky,
and where beneath the ice,
water courses through silver veins
that have no beginning
and no end.

But here, the length and breadth of night

will soon spread like a shroud
over something small and rigid—
something like a heart.

2

Again, they tell her
that her child is dead.
This time more glibly
from white cotton collars
that have forgotten to weep.

But what do these women know about stillbirth?
Bouncing brown-eyed boys and girls,
they fry chicken in aproned rooms.

They do not talk,
for they have learned to coo.
They do not wish,
for wishing has already made it so.

Perhaps she will tell them how—even now—
two small fists sleep like pink snails
in her hands.

3

Every evening, she watches his hands on the knife and fork,
spearing and slicing across the metal plate
as if it were a battlefield.
His head bent to the task,
he makes quick work of it and then drops
the utensils in the center of the plate.

There is no spoon on the table.
A waste, he says.
Why use a spoon when there is bread?

Each evening, she sits with a man who saws and sops.
Like Sisyphus,
you might imagine her happy.

4

In the pasture, she eases into lavender light
as the summer sod browns.

Later as darkness falls,
she will raise her palms to the stars,
the velvet breath of night filling hands
that have killed ten chickens that day.

In this place, the beautiful and the terrible
live like family, sharing a table
and a bed.

5

The voices of women fill the clapboard church.
This is my story, this is my song
Praising my Savior all the day long.

She would join them,
but what can she offer that has not been offered?

Two stillborn children
and twelve bookless years.

6

Tonight, she dreams of lace
and bone china,
of the easy cadence of conversation
filling parlors with papered walls.

Here in gilded frames are generations

under glass: fathers and mothers,
beautiful boys in smart caps and girls
in ribbons.

She dreams that her voice is a bud,
a tight tangle of petals that strain against its center—
then burst,
sending violet words into the room.

7

She could love this place
when the wind tosses the green heads of switchgrass,
when the sun sends notes of larkspur and evening primrose
across the earth.

She could love it when her door opens
to the scent of dirt, rich and ready,
when the sky is a shining cornflower plate
suspended high above the prairie.

And when it is not, she can close her door and wait
until she can love it again.

8

Today, the prairie unfolds before her,
its collar unbuttoned, the skin of its brown throat
exposed.

Through the tall grass, she can feel it stretching
towards the horizon

until the light fades and it unrobes,
the fabric of the day pooling
at its feet.

She might try to stitch it together again,

her fingers, like darning needles, flashing gold
into the darkening expanse.

But this night, as every night,
will unravel before her—
the threads of wind and land undone,
the story of this autumn day
told.

Until dawn
when it will all begin again: a new day
buttoned in the prairie's finest.

Night Sky

Honeyed ribbons of the day hug the horizon
where embers smolder along the ridge.

It's dark, you say,
as you open the barrel of your flashlight
to check for batteries before you walk the path
from the campsite to the lake.

But already I stand at the lake's edge
where constellations of pebbles flicker in the airglow
and waves lap the shore in lunar time.

And above—oh, the too wondrous above—
the sky is a feast of light.
Cassiopeia, Ursa Major and Minor, and stars
which stud the heavens with opal and moonstone.

The universe really puts on a great spread, I say
and take your hand as we walk towards the boat landing.

This is the hand that held the flashlight, long since pocketed,
the hand that now holds mine as if to say:

> Let meteors shower the hills
> and comets blaze in the treetops.
> Let dark become light
> and the moon on the lake our lodestar.
>
> For there is galaxy enough,
> here and now,
> when even the sand is celestial.

Wild Clover

Along the Soap Creek bottoms,
wild clover covers the earth like a violet duvet,
here for a season, gone tomorrow.
These are saffron days
when even in the hollows,
light teases the shadows, unraveling
the dark edges of night.

That this will pass,
that these days will not last
is like a descant that lilts above
the song of seasons.

Like happiness,
that pink-cheeked child who, for a time,
dances with rosehipped abandon
until she returns to earth.

Like love
which crowns the buckthorn
and lays hands upon the brambles.

Like love
whose filaments—slight as cottonwood seeds—
rise until we can see them no more.

Prayer For The Fawns

From a distance, I see a dark shape
at the edge of the road.
A dog, no doubt,
hit by one of the trucks that takes this corner too fast,
trucks that carve smooth ribbons of clay into the new gravel
that the county lays each summer.

Upon nearing, however, I see a smattering of white spots
on a dew-slicked back.
And legs, curled tightly as if womb sleeping,
cocooned in liquid time.

Even in death, there is something expectant here.
As if these legs would unfurl at any moment,
their gleeful joints and sinews stretching,
their bones so perfectly knit together
finding purpose.

Even in death, these ears fold perfectly
into soft crescents at the crown.
I long to run my hand over them
the way a mother smooths a child's hair which spreads
like a silk fan across her pillow at night.
And I long to see the timber—just yards away—
reach its oaken arms to snatch this life
from death.

This is my prayer for the fawns,
for all that would begin.

Bubble Boy

In 1971, David Vetter was born with severe immunodeficiency.
Known as the Bubble Boy, he lived his entire life of 12 years in a
plastic bubble.

Decades ago before you were born,
a boy spent his entire life in a plastic bubble
because the world threatened to take him out
with an arsenal of parasites and plagues.
From his bubble, he could see children, like you,
who ran barefoot in the sun,
their fingers slicked with dirt,
their tongues testing the wind.

Today, you dip your wand into a bucket of solution
and a bubble big as a porpoise takes the air.
It floats several exuberant feet off the grass,
an Aurora borealis here in our own yard.
You step to meet it,
but from the driveway where I stand,
it looks as if you've stepped into it—
or perhaps it's caught you.
And once inside, your face opens in wonder
at a world glazed with color.

Soon you'll poke it and it will burst,
coating your hair with soapy film.
And then you'll come running
through the grass, you'll laugh
and throw yourself, soapy and sweaty,
into your mother's arms.

At six years, suited up like an astronaut,
the Bubble Boy stepped out of his plastic world
into his mother's arms for the first time,

arms that had pined for flesh—skin-to-skin love,
one eager heart pressed to another.
On his eleventh birthday, he asked to see the stars
and they wheeled him into the yard
where—for twenty miraculous minutes—he gazed at the sky.
But at twelve, even the bubble couldn't save him.

Tonight, you'll sit under the stars
by the fire where we've roasted marshmallows.
And later when you fall asleep, your sticky face against your
mother's shoulder,
you'll dream of all the things you want to see
and touch.

Catching A Wave

In early summer, the wind pushes through
the tops of elms and dapples
the road below.
It whips the pastures into waves,
the grasses rolling surely
upon the shore of summer.

This is high tide,
and my heart swells.
What once was dark and brittle
is now a happy vapor, a lemon trifle,
a lark.
Oh, that I might sing the wind's songs,
that I might live in the land of lilac
where prayers are always fragrant,
always weightless.

I grow old.
But today, I feel like riding the waves
of May apple and merrybells.
I feel as though I may go beyond the breakers—
beyond the shoal of age—
into bright danger.

Today, I think I will leave the shallows
where I have hidden among the rocks.
Here, as I am swept out of myself,
I will scatter my all years, like shells,
across the sand.
And then, I will catch the closest wave
and ride hard with the wind.

For Griffin, Almost Five

Three goldfinches sit on a wire.
They punctuate the cornflower sky
like saffron exclamation points.
Look! Look! Look!
Wren-bodied, but mighty,
their golden breasts blaze
in the noonday sun.

These are waifs with heart.
Like you at four-almost-five
with eyes that flash in the spaces between minutes
and hands like hummingbirds
that whip the air.

But you lean into me,
a favorite book between us,
and for a moment, we linger in the land of words,
strolling lines that wrap leisurely from one page
to the next.

Until, fingers aquiver,
you take my hand and pull me out the door.
Look! Look! Look!
Three goldfinches on a wire

and one boy
who punctuates my life.

Honeysuckle Berries

After the storm,
the honeysuckle berries hang cased in ice
like fossils in amber—perfectly themselves,
but suspended in time.

Earlier, these vines were loaded with plump berries
which we squeezed between our fingers,
releasing puddles of yellow juice into our palms.
And before that, branches burst with white-fluted blossoms,
the first fragrance of spring.

Now these vines hold hard, red globes
resistant to finger or nose.
The ice storm has strung a necklace of rubies across the land,
and these gems are strictly for the eyes.

How often it's like that—the things you want to smell and hold
but can't:

> a violet afloat in a paperweight,
> a child too lovely for burial.

School Drop-Off

I hear the first sobs,
but the wind carries them away now.
His head bends into his sister,
and they move—as one child—
toward the school.

It is enough that he leaves
his hat and heart in my hands.
But this!
This promise of return flies,
as it must,
a fierce flag in the space between us.

And his sister who takes him in,
whose hand in his, a small clutch of love,
promises what I cannot:
I am here,
I am right here.

Fifty yards away,
the edges of their silhouette cut me.
This is almost more than I can bear,
this surety that so much life goes on beyond me,
that they will enter the school
and not look back.

Song Of The Cottonwoods

The summer voice of the cottonwoods
lies transparent in baby breaths
on the water.
It floats in faint wisps
in the channels and along the shoreline.

In the evening at the water's edge,
you can dip your hands into the shallows
and catch a whisper,
a syllable of promise.

There is sacredness in words unspoken,
in such fragile potential that moves, as it will,
in the breeze.

And at dawn when the day is a rosy glaze
upon the lake,
there are filaments so fine
that they are lost in light.

This is the song of the cottonwoods.

So This Is Joy

your silk skirt alive,
a deep red river running at your feet;
the gilded grass;
the cottonwood bough which lowers
an unexpected crown;

and a distant tree line squeezing the sun
to the center of the clearing
where it settles into a buttery pat
of light.

So this is joy:
the switchgrass lit with birthday candles
a fiery party for one;

while above, the late afternoon sky pales,
an afterthought.

So this is joy:
arms which open
with minds of their own;
such bounty, such unculled charity,
as if to pull the whole world in—
all its toadstools and troubles—

and you, twirling in the twilight,
your silk cyclone such a magnificent sight,
daring the world to sulk.

The Leap

When twilight eases into the tall grass
and the air groans under its own weight,
a girl leaps
and there on the windless meadow
she hangs suspended
above the foxtail and bushclover.

And the leap—
call it abandon, call it rapture—
splits the plane of possibility.
Arms and legs take the evening by wing,
while gravity lies spent and breathless,
completely undone.

Such an extravagant offering:
the height and breadth of mystery,
this kinder air.

The Sailors Of Cinque Terre

Stacks of houses hold fast
to rocks which fall
straight into the sea.
From your boat,
your eyes move across their graying silhouettes,
which darken, moment by moment,
at dusk.

Until, just as the sun is setting,
a final shaft of light
brings the mountain to pastel life:
terra cotta, saffron, pistachio and pink.
You fix your eyes on the color of your heart
and steer for home.

In the moonlight,
terra cotta, saffron,
pistachio and pink sing like sirens
beckoning you home.

What Will Hold

In late July, bare-chested
you cast your line from the dock
that you fear—that you have *always* feared—
will not hold you.

Its cedar has weathered beyond its natural life.
Month after month, it loses all that was level and plumb,
and its bones, taut and gnarled,
are desperate to hold the center
whose sagging belly has begun to surrender itself
to the water.

But still you stand,
eyes fixed on the red and white bobber
which floats motionless on the green surface.
You wonder if the surface will hold,
if your little bobber will sun with confidence
in those precious fishing minutes before supper—
or if a bass will suck it violently
into the dense forests of moss below.

As you shift your weight,
the dock grumbles and grouses beneath you.
You move closer to the edge
where you have found that the planks don't protest
as much.
And then you look out to the road
which curls assuredly around the pond to home.

Here is a gravel mooring for your soul.
Here, in this summer moment,
you step from the edge into the center,
where the dock, the day, and the world
hold.

Witching Hour At Lake Wapello

At dusk,
lily pads which crowd the shoreline
pocket the last light.
We sit on the bank and watch as clouds
press the final mauve moments of day
into the distant hills.

Night threatens to take it all—
the lake, the hills, us—
in one deep blue mouthful.

But this is the witching hour
where minutes, like lily pads, spread leisurely
across the lake.
This is the twixt time
when water winks in color.

Anything is possible,
everything lives to dream again.
The earth below us
holds the warmth of the day longer than it should,
and we fall back into its arms,
bewitched and dumb.

What can we say that hasn't been said?

Our words are snails
beneath the algae bloom.
Tonight, we carol among cattails,
strolling the shore like loons.

Swinging

These are feet I know well.
Ten button toes stuffed,
too often, into unnecessary shoes.

They've walked the path from
your house to mine so many times
that even the creeping charlie has given up
and left a red clay artery to harden
in the sun.

Shoeless today, they take to the air,
dangling dreamily from the swing in the big oak,
their bottoms coated with dirt
even before noon.

Again, you say.
And I push again with all that I have
because I remember how the swing's chains would squeak—
then catch—
when I'd gone as high as I could;
when, with each pass,
I took to the sky as a swallow;
when my hair would find the breeze
and I'd close my eyes because it was better this way,
the rising and falling taking my gut
by surprise.

I push hard, running beneath you,
hoping to tease the air into taking you further into the oak boughs,

hoping to catch you by the feet so that I can release you
again.

The Smallest Girl

In the Blue Moon Valley near Lijiang, China, legend has it that
when a boy and girl fall in love, the boy must be tested by standing
with bare feet in the river during winter. This act reveals his
commitment to his beloved, and locals believe this love will live
eternally in the presence of the holy snow mountain.

At the beginning of the Yuan Dynasty,
the smallest girl kneels beside the turquoise waters
of the Blue Moon Valley.
She plunges her hands into the current
where they dance for a moment
and then still, numb with cold.

Along the Ancient Tea Horse Road, others walk and sing
offering themselves to the mountains
which rise above the valley like white dragons.

But the smallest girl can neither see nor hear them.
Her eyes swim like ancient carp in the deepest pools,
and her ears are stone lockets.

Each evening when stars sequin the earth,
she cries:

> *Where is the mother to braid my hair?*
> *Where are the brothers and sisters who share plums at*
> *noon?*
> *Where are the doors to shut out the cold?*

The smallest girl weeps for soft hands, plum joy, and strong doors,
but these are the ghosts of dragonflies which dip,
stirring the water's surface and then disappear—
too eager for the sun.

In the violet shadow of the mountains, others sit
and listen to the ancient voices:

> *He who loves a girl*
> *will stand with bare feet*
> *on the stones of the sacred river.*
> *He will speak her name and give himself*
> *to cold and time.*
> *And she will know his heart*
> *and the love that bears all.*

Oh, the smallest girl longs to curl her hands into
mossy palms, to nest them forever
in this cache of love!
But her fingers are spruce needles glazed with ice,
and they pine with lucent spears that cut
the night.

Season after season,
the sun and the moon winter her dreams.
Yet at the river's edge in the Blue Moon Valley,
the smallest girl sings such songs
to make the stones cry out.

To My Mother On Her 86th Birthday

For years, he wrapped his best gift
into a single sheet of typing paper
and tucked it in the corner of your vanity mirror.
And there, your husband's words,
like spring's first crocus,
pushed their snowy heads eagerly
into the gray days of winter.
Each birthday, they took careful root in the only
seed bed worth tending.

To his best reader,
to the love—oh, the love of his life!
To the home he carried with him,
into and out of the dark places that might have undone him,
but for you.
To the one who makes do, who takes little
and gives much.
To the loveliest of all the birds he kept,
the one whose silver wings flash like bright berries
in the junipers.

And now the words are left to me.
I can hear my father's fingers on his Royal typewriter,
the quick slap of thumb and forefingers,
the blue rush of each carriage return.
I can feel the round keys give themselves, as they must,
to a rhythm preordained.
And the small metal stand with wings that unfold
to hold notebooks and such
quakes with each image pounded into life.

Now, the words he gifted—
so many words spilling from line to line,
jumping the white spaces of the decades—

jumping the white spaces of the decades—
now, this word cache strains against the grave.

And so, on your birthday,
consider this a single page tucked into the corner
of your vanity.
Consider that the old black Royal lumbers on
with humble words unearthed from the genetic soil
of the one who loves you
always.

Fireflies

As a child, I combed the yard for fireflies
and dropped them into Mason jars
with holes punched in the lids.
For a while, they didn't disappoint.
I held the jar into the night sky and watched
my catch flash against the glass.

But in the morning, those that lived
had sad brown bellies like common beetles,
and I dumped them into the grass.

Tonight, I drive home in a meteor shower.
The fireflies smear my windshield with phosphorescence
and seed the ditches with sequins.

Their abdomens ignite with love
and a Morse code of light takes the fields,
dots and dashes coupling wildly
in the dark.

Even if you offer me a field-sized Mason jar
or a host of hybrids guaranteed to shine for life,
I'll pass.

I'll say,

> *Pull over and watch the show.*
> *It only runs for a few more weeks.*

And then we'll feast our eyes on fields aflicker
until we have to leave.

From The Air

our beach is a continent
pushing its way into the sea,
which is really a lake—
and not a large lake at that—

but you wouldn't know this from the air
where an expanse of blue wraps around
a bone-colored peninsula, and moss crowds in
like a barrier reef.

From the air, an entire world lies here:
a body of water, a landform,
and us.

And yet in Pieter Brueghel's famous painting,
you can't take your eyes off the water and land,
that glittering ocean and fertile field.
You have to look long to see the boy, Icarus,
who drowns in the lower corner
where two white legs enter the water
without notice.

From the air today, a turquoise sea shimmers below
where the beach intercedes like an afterthought.
And in the center of it all, we lie:

two white limbs.

House Of Common Prayer

Near the edge of the timber
where a ravine cuts a deep swath in the clay,
a stand of yellow clover rises,
one bright chapel in the brome.

This is a house of common prayer,
my matins,
where I lay my wood sorrel at the altar
and weave my voiceless psalms
among the birdsong.

This is a place of rest,
safe from thistle and teasel;
a place of hand-folding, green-knuckled
and small;
a place where the length of oxtongue is lament,
and the depth of dandelion
is praise.

I have been here before
as a child who traveled alleys
and once found—keeping vigil behind the corner grocery store —
a hallelujah of hollyhocks.

Even at eight, I knew this was a place of prayer,
that there behind the garbage cans were crimson blossoms
preparing a way in the wilderness.

Marmalade Moon

As the moon rises
it spreads marmalade across the treetops.

Too often, the world is a wafer
broken easily by brittle words.
But tonight, we who live lean
stand dumb in the presence
of such decadence:

a light feast,
a banquet of lunar nectar.

In this month of marmalade moons
we remember how the world ripens;
how the sweet peach of summer swallows
all our pits and stones;
how we rest in the nectarine assurance that—
if even for a moment—
there is enough for all.

My Mother's Raincoat

was nothing but a 2-ply, black
plastic garbage bag
with a single hole punched through
for her head.

And huddled in the McCook High School bleachers,
beside another mother
who, too, had grown into such a poncho,
she watched the Girl's District Track Meet
below.

It was spring in Nebraska,
and the northwest wind blew in sleet from Wyoming,
pelted the garbage bags
and the cotton sweat suits of runners
in the infield.

Beneath green sun visors
keeping drizzle from their eyes,
my mother and her friend looked on
and waved.

And standing alone
at the start of the 440 yard run,
I fumbled to undo the string of my sweatpants.
The lucky beads I always wore around my neck
were not there, and there was nothing
but cold to hold me up.

Until I saw my mother's garbage bag
and remembered that tucked beneath it,
she kept graham crackers and Hershey bars,
Chapstick and peppermints.
Underneath all that wind-whipped plastic

were hands that would rub out the cold
and drive me home.
Underneath it all—
and in spite of the sneers from other runners
who laughed long at the sight of two women in bags—
was the mother who, years later, would stand on the front terrace,
curbside, who would wave until
I turned the corner, and she could see me
no more.

Will she ever know the times I circled the block,
hoping that she hadn't yet gone inside,
hoping to see her waving again,
huddled beneath another makeshift poncho,
a single note of clear, green light
falling through her visor.

On A Second Viewing Of The Pietà

I notice that Mary is disproportionately large—
beautiful, but in truth,
a herculean Madonna who holds the son of God
with one arm only.

Her other arm, however, opens to us all
as if to say *What now?*
as if to say *How now shall we live?*

Here is her palm—open—
the emptiness of which is both beautiful
and terrible.
Her robe is more like baby's swaddling
than a mother's shroud.

And Jesus lies in his mother's lap
much smaller than I'd imagined,
a savior dwarfed by his marble mother.
His head lolls against Mary's sturdy arm;
while his own arms, slack and useless, hang
like afterthoughts.
And his chest (oh, his chest!)
is a chevron of bones and stripes.

In this moment between death and life,
this interminable space between dark and light,
see how his mother holds herself like a mountain,
like a sacred and stony peak.

On a second viewing of the Pietà,
I can't tear my eyes away from all
that is hidden here:

those 33 years lived as boys and young men will,

those countless days marked by a mother's bliss:
the child of her heart at home still,
his place at the table assured,
and the bread broken at each meal,
the labor of her hands.

If I could split this stony silence,
surely I would find a cache of days and joys—
this son laughing,
this mother singing,
their love, like yeast, rising.

Days before my children and grandchildren will gather
at my table, the turkey carved and thanks given,
I stand before this quarry of love and loss

blessed.

Photo Shoot

Your pink tulle skirt catches
in the late summer grass
and for a moment,
the prairie holds you captive.
As if a sleeping seed awakened,
sliding, shooting upward, breaking
the earth's skin and standing tall,
one honey-haired blossom
among the wild chicory and blue stem.

Your mother moves towards you
pressing her eye to the camera.
Surely she sees what I do—
your childhood untethering here
each gossamer piece catching the breeze
and escaping, petal by petal,
into this sacristy of late July.

I long to frame this legacy of loveliness:
a mother's soft eyes,
a daughter's well-kept heart,
both eager to unfurl themselves into time
forever backlit by a golden and forgiving sun.

But even as I try to hold the moment,
I see the light casting long shadows from the tree line,
burnishing pink to mauve.
And so I vow to celebrate the evening,
the hour in which you bloomed so brightly
that I could not mourn the child
you were.

Good Planks

The old barn lists
in a field of sumac.
The seams of its hull have eased
into a hole on the north side.
But from the south,
its planks are good.
From the south,
it is an ark whose girth spreads wide
across a hillside of switchgrass and yarrow.

So it is with you.
Three rows behind you in the theater,
I can't see your head.
Your back which age has bent into the seat
leaves only a wedge of velvet collar
in the fading light.
From the rear, it seems your flesh has given in,
your molecules spilling into and out of this place.

But when I leave, I turn to see that from the front,
your planks are good.
From the front, your hands are locusts
that hum in your lap,
and your eyes, two bright marbles,
search the room like wild cats.

Deliverer

I will raise my cup of deliverance and invoke the Lord's name.
Psalm 116:13

Outside, the world grays.
Bone-weary and lean,
trees reach with brittle fingers that break the sky.
The stalks of Black-eyed Susans bear heads like spiny sea urchins
and the white souls of pampas grass sing hoary carols
along every road.

Everything waits for deliverance from the bondage
of these days:
finches whose once-gold wings now tarnish the frozen air,
capless acorns which litter the timber floor,
clouds which collapse in thin, pale ribbons
upon the horizon.

Everything waits to be delivered—
for a shot of chlorophyll to the heart,
for a familiar chorus of crocus
and thickets laced with light.

Yet even in our exile,
the lichens prostrate themselves
on the backs of sleeping stones.
And wakened with the green hope of fungi,
the stones cry out:
Behold, our Deliverer!

Tree Rut

In November
on the Soap Creek Bottoms,
the tree rut begins.
Shagbark hickories lock limbs
in a tangle of tines.

If you walk through the timber,
you can see them.
Their cork sloughed off and cambium dried up,
they fight for earth and air
like bucks in heat.
Long after their roots have been exposed
with brittle fingers left to claw the cold,
they hold fast—
insistent and unyielding.

And so we wait,
our eyes fixed on this snarl of limb and loss,
our ears tuned to the death rattle.

Soon, snow will cover the timber floor
with all its carnage and decay.
But the hickories will fight on—
their bleached bones a requiem
for the rut.

The River Of Cottonwoods

Before the first frost,
the cottonwood trees unfurl their waxy leaves,
waving them like silver scales
into the light and shadow.
They jewel the sky.
And if you close your eyes,
the wind through the leaves makes the sound of water
coursing over stones.

If you stand alone in a copse of cottonwood,
you can give yourself to this current:
a gift to rival the gold, persimmon, and ochre
that hardwoods lay at the feet of winter's king.

If you stand alone, still and open,
you can let the liquid words of truth
wash over you, eroding all that you were—
each cosmetic layer of something bright
but false,
the shale of pride ground to sediment
and deposited like silt on the forest floor.

This is autumn's baptism:
leaves and wind and water,
a rite performed by tree fathers.
What can you do but enter this river,
without guile or rudder?

The Day The Indigo Bunting Showed Up

The day the indigo bunting showed up at the feeder
was a good day.
All my life, I'd been waiting,
   waiting,
     waiting.

All my life, I'd been scanning the tree line
for any flash of blue, only to find
common jays that tricked the eye.

And oh, the things that trick the eye!
        words with rose-breasted bellies;
        cads who fly their honeyed hearts
        from field to hive;
        and armies of intentions marching gloriously
        to nowhere.

How I've been dazzled
by the world's fine sheen,
my eyes fixed too often
on castles and baubles.

But this was no trick,
this moment of blue beyond
imagining.
Dumbstruck, I stood before the window
eager that I might move closer,
wishing that I might show up
with just as much sapphire certainty.

On the day the indigo bunting arrived,
I marveled that I had eyes to see.

Sumac

The county crews have poisoned the sumac.
Around each utility pole, it makes a last stand:
an army of scarlet fury
amidst the season's last green.
The roadside is ablaze with autumn
come too soon.
Summer's arteries have burst,
spilling its life-blood through the land.

I drive to town
and cannot keep my eyes on the road.
To my right and left, carmine and crimson,
garnet and currant fill the ditches.
There is such beauty in this dying.
If you roll down your windows,
you can hear the song of sumac,
a bright, expectant elegy that soars across the fields.

Here among the sumac,
I would like to make my last stand:
a fiery finish glorious enough
to stop traffic.

The Passion Of November

Here is a green that is gold,
a sacrifice of leaf to limb.

I kneel at the foot of ash and elm
and my tears seed the earth
with longing.

I look up
into arms outstretched, their palms open
in the midday sun.

Below me,
the fecund matter of the saints
lies in burnished piles.

In the ditches,
I rub shoulders with grasses
and milkweed grown tall.

And into the chill,
vaporous at first, but surer then
the limbs speak:

> *Woman, behold your son.*
> *Son, behold your mother.*

Here in the absence of green
I take bronze to my breast.

This is the passion of November.

Sunrise, Late September

The rosy underbelly of the clouds
descends in a watercolor wash upon the hills
sending pink light into the fields.

Here is the sweet spot.
Here time, in all its translucence,
turns the present into memory and vision,
each palpable and almost visible.
Here, the imperceptible floats in the breeze
just beyond your reach.

In late September when colors run at dawn,
you hold what has been and what will be,
upon your outstretched palm.
And there, with wings spun silver,
they quiver and take flight.

Late Autumn, Southern Iowa

What green is left
lies muted beneath a veil of frost.
Its voice, caught in the throat of autumn,
is silent.

The wild parsnip and chicory are gone.
The linden and cottonwood loose their hair,
sending mounds of russet strands to the ground.

But what of this fodder?
What of these silos of dry bones and song?
In a season soon to sleep,
how now shall we live?
In a season soon to sleep,
who will speak the truth of green?

For white is not absence;
its presence is a crushing thing
that runs its mouth with colder claims.

So who will speak the truth of green,
its blooms and dreams,
its primrose promise of return?

Last Mowing

After the last mowing,
the grasses shorn nearly to the earth along Mink Road,
the Queen Anne's Lace blooms quickly.
The slender stems hold bridal bonnets
on doll-sized versions of their summer selves.
At three or four inches, they are no less lovely
than they were in late June.
In the early days of September,
they refuse to give in, refuse to welcome the autumn
that is sure to come.

I walk with my head lowered.
I can't get enough of these tiny soldiers
who muscle through grass clippings and roadside waste.
These are September's heroes who have forgotten their place,
who insist on singing even as the cottonwoods and maples
drop their leaves.

Today is not a good day to die, they say.
Today, the world is not enough without us.
Today, we sing.

Cardinal In Late Winter

The day breaks over a monochrome world
where there is only the memory
of color.

I've had enough of gray:
of pasty trees too weak to shoulder the sky;
of hills, like lumps of coal, that clot the earth;
of skies that slather the sun for weeks.

Even my dreams plod through the nights
dragging their shrouds across the land.
They sober in the company of stones
as their eyes are sealed and their tongues
removed.

Outside, the world writes its obituary—
line by leaden line—
and the snow is a hearse through the streets
of my days.

But in the linden,
a solitary cardinal.

And suddenly,
it's as if the world remembers its better self,
as if it can sing in scarlet again.
Here is red resurrected:
we sink our teeth into it,
and sweet juice runs from our lips;
we breathe it in, and languid moments blossom;
we look into the eyes of vermillion and rose
and smile.

The monochrome world presses in,

but a single cardinal takes the day.

Sierra Madre Range, Wyoming

Which of you, if your son asks for bread, will give him a stone?
Matthew 7:9

Long ago,
the earth opened its vault
and offered its best stones,
granite memories of younger days
before mountain juniper seeded the slopes.

In wagons and pushing handcarts,
the pioneers may have dreamt of an unleavened trail,
may have opened their hands and asked for bread
as they pressed towards the promised land.
But the earth gave them stones which still roam the land
like leviathans, their backs being broken—season after season—
by wind and water.

Their hooded eyes fixed on the ground below,
they troll the mountain side.
They jut and they jeer;
they threaten to break free.
Even the sage quakes at their feet.

Yet, what a glacial offering, this bounty of boulders
and how the earth turns its face to the sun
and sings:

Let them eat stones.

Round Bales

The round bales sit in frosted fields,
relics of summer, now dried and resting
under a slate sky.

From the road, some think *straw.*
But they miss the mystery at the center,
still green, still germinating,
a glorious nucleus,
a promise of pastures with hair thrown
heedlessly into the breeze.

So it is with all ordinary mysteries,
their burlap coats buttoned over tender miracles
which take refuge in the dark.

Until one with nimble fingers
unravels each layer,
picks a way through the chaff and chill.

Then the center exhales
its warm breath escaping across the earth,
its timbre taking shape.

The round bales sit as tombs.
Yet even now, their stones are being rolled away,
their life source redeemed.

All The Best Things

are smaller than we imagine.

Think of acorns with their wee brown caps;
pieces of bottle glass hidden in the gravel,
their edges worn smooth enough to pocket;

of snowdrops and their paper white blossoms—
but think smaller still
to the embroidery of green that hems
each petal.

Think of wrinkles that run like tributaries
from your grandmother's eyes:
such rare, fine lines spilling into
the delta of her life;

of all those frothy seeds that catch the breeze
and how silently they travel,
how they make a way
without fuss.

Think of the moment inside a moment,
the nucleus of your time here.

Think smaller than you've ever dared—

and even smaller still.

Goldfinch In Winter

Even winter, that great robber
of all things gold and good
cannot take this:

the way the snow is a winter scrim,

the way your onyx wings beat it
until the season softens

and the whole white world lays its specter
before you.

April Day

This is how I'll remember you
when my day is wrinkled and slow,
when there's news of all sorts of ugliness
and the world is a troll,

I'll remember how your brother looked into your eyes
and found a constellation of joy,
how the green breath of spring moved through the elms
and even the horseweed was lovely.

I'll remember how he reached for you with hopeful hands,
and how you bent your head to his and offered all:
    a cornflower sky
    a bright field
    an open heart.

Then how his smile ravished the meadow
sending tansy and trillium dashing through the woods
to take the morning by storm.

This is how I'll remember you
when my days and nights lie fallow
and age takes me to the mat:

I'll remember you in April,
green and tender,
with eyes only for each other.

Apple Blossom Time
—for Gracyn

For months, winter has cast
stern silhouettes upon the land—
such spears and snarls,
twigs and tines
to make the hours weep.

Until spring simply opens the world, releasing
baskets of balloons which take the air
with saffron joy.
Until the first sweet blossoms pink the day,
blushing against the cornflower sky.

Tomorrow, you will turn eleven.
But for months, you've been pruning
the branches of childhood,
making space for something even brighter
in the canopy above.

Now, the first blooms begin to peek around
the corners of innocence.
They test the breeze,
their petals pearl with dew.

This is apple blossom time,
this liminal space where girlhood smiles
one last rosy smile, and minutes blink
in wonder.

This is apple blossom time,
when the world is pinker, softer

and you, my darling bud, are lovelier
than you know.

Love Story

I look west.

There is a single hole
in the clouds through which
time is escaping.

—Don Welch, "The River, for Dutch Welch"

Come with me
and lift the scarlet hands of oaks
higher, wilder,
ever towards the sky.

Come with me
and move across the fecund timber floor
on moccasins.

Autumn's emerald curtain is still drawn
against the hills.
Here among the wood ferns and wild ginger,
house wrens exhale,
their songs lambent with chlorophyll.
Here, lichens whisper into the pale ochre light,
their words eager and expectant.

Here is your love story:
the emerald and scarlet,
the damp assurance of all that is true,

and sunlight through a single porthole—
one sweet breach into the grand overstory
beyond.

End Roll
—*for my mother*

It's a gift from the newspaper office, you say—
an end roll of newsprint on a spool
that stands 3 feet tall on its cardboard spine—
free for the taking.

All yours, you say,
and I watch as the center cannot hold,
as paper begins to unspool itself
like yarn from a wild skein.

At first, I can't bring myself to put pencil to paper.
The white field before me is too dear.

But even at twelve,
I understand the invitation before me.
The furrows of my palms loosen,
and then I begin to draw what I've only imagined—
tentative at first, but then surer—

until I've given form to an acre of possibilities
until I've drawn right up to the cardboard core.

I'm still the one who trembles before paper,
the one who finds the world on the back of an envelope,
whose hours are lost and gained
when my pen finds its way.

I was born a fallow field
where shapeless, wordless things would incubate,
the loam of my lifetime deeper and richer because
even before I knew this,

you knew.

We Would Be Poorer

The worth of these trees can be described negatively: without them, we would be poorer.
——margin notes from Don Welch on
W. C. Williams' "The Botticellian
Trees"

Finally, the purple souls of crocus unfurl themselves
into the April sun,
and lumbering from the depths,
catfish whisker their way to the surface;

violets ring the timber again,
and resurrected at the base of dead elms,
morels push through the strata of leaves,
their yellow heads drowsy and damp
with dew.

Without them, we would be poorer.

My grandson's stories have wings,
and as he tells them, they always find a tailwind.
At home at once in easy air, they plot a gallant course
and refuse to come down;

my father's books have margins of musing;
on each page, a geography of words hems the borders
and here, the lexicon of his life
marvels through precious inches
of white space.

Without them, we would be poorer.

The way you love me from beyond.
The way you reach across the years
to find that smooth-cheeked girl who had yet to know
the knots and gnarls of life:

   how the sinews of her dreams could atrophy;
   how, in the end, she would stop running,
   the race already won.

Without you, I would be poorer.

About the Author

For as long as Shannon Vesely can remember, the dining room table in her family home has been a genuine place of higher education and moral development. As the dishes were cleared and her family settled in for hours of good talk, she learned how to love language, to see the extraordinary in the ordinary, to listen with the best ears, and to think her way towards wisdom. For forty-one years, she spent her days in classrooms where she sought to bring these gifts to thousands of students throughout the Midwest. Retired now, Shannon reads avidly, writes poetry, as well as a weekly blog, and spends as much time with her grandchildren as she can. Her father, poet Don Welch, claimed that we all have at least "one good poem in our hidden heads." She writes with the continued hope of uncovering her one "good poem."

Acknowledgements

It goes without saying that my parents, Don and Marcia Welch, have taught me most of what I know about parenting, teaching, writing, and living. I'd like to thank them for creating and sustaining a home filled with language and love. How blessed I've been and continue to be as a result of their love and encouragement.

Made in the USA
Monee, IL
30 October 2021

81095184R00046